T0029185

FOR AUNT MARIANNE,
A CONSTANT GUIDING LIGHT IN MY LIFE
—A.C.R.

FOR PENNY AND SADIE
—E.S.

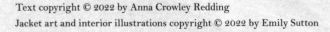

Text copyright © 2022 by Anna Crowley Redding
Jacket art and interior illustrations copyright © 2022 by Emily Sutton

All rights reserved. Published in the United States by Random House Studio,
an imprint of Random House Children's Books, a division of Penguin Random House LLC, New York.
Random House Studio with colophon is a trademark of Penguin Random House LLC.

Visit us on the Web! rhcbooks.com
Educators and librarians, for a variety of teaching tools, visit us at RHTeachersLibrarians.com

Library of Congress Cataloging-in-Publication Data is available upon request.
ISBN 978-0-593-37340-8 (trade)
ISBN 978-0-593-37341-5 (lib. bdg.)
ISBN 978-0-593-37342-2 (ebook)

The illustrations in this book were rendered in watercolor, ink, pencil, and pastel.
The text of this book is set in 15-point Bell MT Pro.
Interior design by Rachael Cole

MANUFACTURED IN CHINA
10 9 8 7 6 5 4 3 2 1
First Edition

Random House Children's Books supports the First Amendment and celebrates the right to read.

Penguin Random House LLC supports copyright. Copyright fuels creativity, encourages diverse voices, promotes free speech, and creates a vibrant culture. Thank you for buying an authorized edition of this book and for complying with copyright laws by not reproducing, scanning, or distributing any part in any form without permission. You are supporting writers and allowing Penguin Random House to publish books for every reader.

Courage Like Kate

THE TRUE STORY OF A GIRL LIGHTHOUSE KEEPER

WRITTEN BY

Anna Crowley Redding

ILLUSTRATED BY

Emily Sutton

RANDOM HOUSE STUDIO ▲ NEW YORK

Fayerweather Island had seen blustery, bone-chilling blizzards.
It had seen rip-roaring rising tides and wicked windswept waves.
Yet it had never seen a pint-sized hurricane—until five-year-old
Kate Moore claimed that tiny island as her own.

It may not have been more than a sliver of sandy rock slicing through the surf, but there was room for a garden, farm animals, and best of all, a lighthouse. And Papa was the new lighthouse keeper!

Kate was supposed to be the lighthouse keeper's daughter.

But Kate thought of herself as Papa's assistant.

Wherever Papa went, so did Kate.

Whatever Papa did, so did Kate.

She learned how to sow and grow a garden,

shepherd and shear
the sheep,

milk the cows,

collect the eggs,

and catch rainwater
for drinking.

And when greedy gales grabbed gobs of sand to steal Fayerweather back
into the sound, Kate planted tree after tree to root her island in rock.

By the time Kate turned twelve years old, there was still one job she had not conquered: tending the lighthouse alone. And truth be told, those thirty-three steep, spiraling stairs up the lighthouse tower took their toll on Papa's body. Captain Moore needed Kate's help.

Kate knew the walk was dark, the work was difficult, and the weather was treacherous. She knew the lighthouse's staircase was torturous. She knew the wee hours were tedious. Each dangerous duty was everything that little girls in the 1800s were not supposed to do. After all, women were told they were absolutely, positively not capable of such bravery, courage, or strength. Little girls were supposed to be ladylike, not lighthouse keepers.

But Kate thought about her father, and she thought about the ships under sail that needed the light for safety. And that's when she traded in her skirt for a pair of pants and got to work.
Kate may not have been the official lighthouse keeper.
But she was the girl for the job.

Clutching her lantern, Kate felt the sting of salt spray hit her eyes. It took six hundred steps to make it from the keeper's house to the tower. Kate searched the dark for the rickety wooden walkway that led to the lighthouse. The glow of her lamplight revealed ice-coated planks.

One wrong move and Kate would fall off the boards
and into the icy water sloshing beneath her feet. Tap.
She felt for her next step. Tap. Tap.

CREEAK.

Kate pried open the heavy door of the lighthouse and filled her bucket with whale oil.

CLANG. CLANG. CLANG.

Stepping on every iron tread, her ice-cold feet set the rhythm for her climb. She lugged the heavy bucket in one hand and carried her lantern in the other all the way to the top.

Kate eyed the ladder hanging
from the ceiling. One last climb.
Hooking the pail in the crook of
her arm, Kate wrestled her way up
each rung until she reached the
trapdoor.

She pushed it open and crawled
inside the lantern room.

Waves thundered. Windows rattled. Kate poured whale oil into all eight lamps.

Snip. Snip. Snip. She trimmed the wicks as the thick cotton strings soaked up the oil.

Then Kate set them alight.

The burning white light chased away
shadows, illuminated ship-crushing rocks,
and pointed the way to safe harbor.

Kate retraced each shaky step all the way home. Crawling into bed, Kate knew it was just for a nap. She had three more trips to make. After all, to keep the light ablaze, the oil would need to be refilled every four hours.

But some nights, the fierce fury of storms pushed howling winds through every nook and cranny of the tower, snuffing out the light after Kate kindled the flames. Kate had no choice but to sit next to the lanterns all night long, relighting them each time the wind turned the lighthouse dark.

She trained her ear to listen. No matter how loud the SQUAWK of an osprey, the SHRIEK of a gale, or the ROAR of the waves, Kate could hear even the faintest cry for help.

Night after night, launching her boat into the
black water, she rowed toward those cries.
    *Papa had taught her how to handle an oar
better than any man could.*

Time after time, miles from shore, Kate raced
to pull men to safety.

*Papa had taught her how to keep the boat steady
when snatching seamen from swirling swells.*

Year after year, she sailed wind-whipped seas and clamored over
ice-covered rocks to save half-frozen shipwreck survivors.

Papa had taught her how to nurse them back to health.

Each time, the men could hardly believe it. They had been saved from death—by a WOMAN!

Word of the rescues hit newspapers across the country.

"Heroic!" they called her.

"Heart of a lion," they said.

One fall day, at almost a hundred years old, Papa died. Now,
completely alone, Kate could not imagine leaving her island.
Kate wanted to carry on her work.

So she applied for Papa's job to become the *official* lighthouse keeper of Fayerweather Island.

For forty-seven years, she had grown the gardens, sheared the sheep, milked the cows, tended the light, and saved lives.

And now? Kate worried, wondered, and waited for word.

That Christmas, Kate's name hit the newspapers once again. **READ ALL ABOUT IT!** Kate Moore was finally appointed the *official* lighthouse keeper of Fayerweather Island.

But she had *always* been the woman for the job.

And the twenty-three sailors Kate had plucked from death owed their lives to the once pint-sized heroine who claimed that tiny island as her own.

Extra! Extra! Read All About It!

Kathleen Andre Moore's lighthouse salary was $500 a year. That would be the equivalent of making $13,000 a year today.

It's hard to imagine, but in addition to tending the light, raising food and livestock, and caring for her feeble parents, Kate started two successful businesses.

Kate took advantage of Fayerweather Island's expansive oyster beds by seeding, harvesting, and selling oysters. Her business boomed. And if anyone tried to steal her oysters, she rowed out in her little boat and ordered them to move! Kate told a reporter late in her life that she feared no man.

Long and lonely nights required Kate to stay in the lantern room to keep the light burning, so she spent her downtime carving duck decoys out of blocks of wood. When hunters discovered her work, they bought them by the barrelful.

Kate lived out her retirement in Black Rock, Connecticut, now part of Bridgeport. Her home had a view of the lighthouse.

When asked about the number of lives she saved, Kate responded, "I wish it had been double that number."

Courtesy of the Bridgeport History Center, Bridgeport Public Library

Kathleen Andre Moore
toward the end of her life

Kate Moore Timeline

circa 1812—Kathleen Andre Moore is born.

1817—Kate's father, Stephen Moore, is appointed lighthouse keeper to Black Rock Light on Fayerweather Island.

April 8, 1851—An article about Kate Moore hits newspapers across the country. Kate tells reporters she has saved twenty-one lives so far.

June 13, 1860—Newspapers report another daring rescue, this time of two sailors. Kate sailed two miles from shore and found them holding on to the keel of their capsized sailboat. This rescue brings the known total of people who Kate saved to twenty-three.

1871—Kate's father dies. Kate is finally named the official lighthouse keeper at the age of fifty-nine.

1878—Kate Moore retires.

February 7, 1899—Kathleen Andre Moore dies at eighty-six years old.

May 12, 2014—The Coast Guard names a fast response cutter *Kathleen Moore.*

AUTHOR'S NOTE

In the late summer of 2014, I traveled to the lighthouse to speak with local historians and discovered that some special schoolchildren were volunteering their time to paint over graffiti on the tower, pick up litter, and learn about Kate's heroism.

As it turned out, this was an important part of their healing process. They had been students at Sandy Hook Elementary School in Newtown, Connecticut, which suffered a terrible tragedy on December 14, 2012. In memory of their six-year-old friend Ben Wheeler, who died that day, the survivors adopted this motto: Helping Is Healing. Choosing Kate's lighthouse as their community service project was inspired by Ben's love of lighthouses.

VISIT

You can visit Fayerweather Island in Bridgeport, Connecticut, today. The lighthouse still stands. The top of Kate's tower is a favorite nesting spot for osprey.

SELECTED BIBLIOGRAPHY

Associated Press. "Life-saving Lighthouse Keeper Honored." May 8, 2014.
    bigstory.ap.org/article/life-saving-lighthouse-keeper-honored.

Cincinnati Daily Press. "A Courageous Girl Saves Two Lives." June 25, 1860: 1.

Moore, Kathleen A. *Journal of Lighthouse Station at Black Rock.* March 3, 1871–January 29, 1878.
    Handwritten. Bridgeport Public Library Collection, Bridgeport, CT.

New York Sunday World. "A Lifetime at a Lighthouse." 1889: n. pag.

The Sun (New York). "The Lighthouse Woman." March 24, 1878: 6.

Black Rock Lighthouse on Fayerweather Island, Bridgeport, Connecticut

Lighthouse photos courtesy of the author